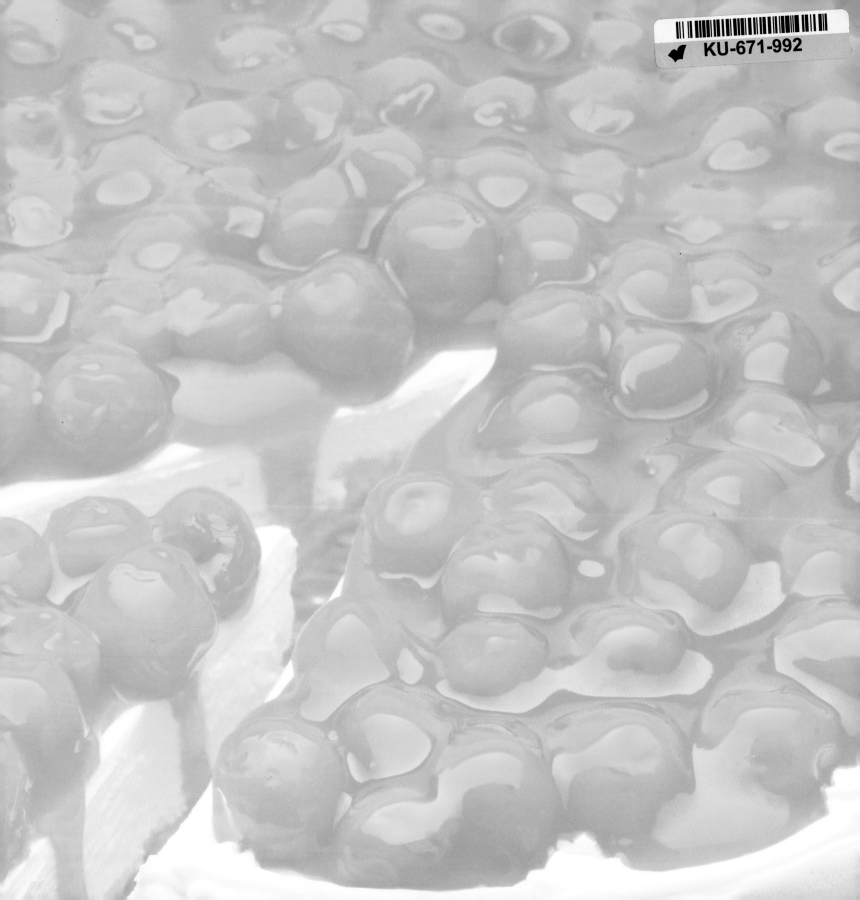

comfort *food*

Marks and Spencer p.l.c.
PO Box 3339
Chester CH99 9QS
www.marksandspencer.com
T21/8283/5311 C.I.F A-37002516

Created and produced by *The Bridgewater Book Company Ltd.*

ISBN: 1-84461-159-0

Printed in China

NOTES FOR THE READER

This book uses both metric and imperial measurements. Follow the same units of measurement throughout; do not mix metric and imperial. All spoon measurements are level: teaspoons are assumed to be 5 ml, and tablespoons are assumed to be 15 ml. Unless otherwise stated, milk is assumed to be full fat, eggs and individual vegetables such as potatoes are medium and pepper is freshly ground black pepper. The times given are an approximate guide only, and may vary according to the techniques and equipment used by different people.

Recipes using raw or very lightly cooked eggs should be avoided by infants, the elderly, pregnant women, convalescents and anyone suffering from an illness. Pregnant and breastfeeding women are advised to avoid eating peanuts and peanut products.

contents

INTRODUCTION   4

CHAPTER 1   8
week days: chill out / TV dinners

CHAPTER 2   32
rainy days: blues chasers

CHAPTER 3   52
lazy weekends

CHAPTER 4   74
childhood favourites

CHAPTER 5   94
chocolate therapy

INDEX   112

introduction

It's been a long day, the bus was late, it's raining and you forgot your umbrella. Time to shut out the world and retreat to the cosiness and reassurance of your own home.

We've all had days like that, and there cannot be many better antidotes than a warming bowl of home-made soup or an indulgent slice of chocolate cake. All too often, however, we settle for a delivery pizza because summoning up the energy to cook 'real' food seems like too much effort. With this book, the problem is solved. It features recipes

that are easy to prepare, use widely available ingredients and are often made in minutes. Above all, they offer that great intangible – the comfort factor.

It's not just on days when everything goes wrong that we seek solace in such meals. Sometimes everything has gone right but it's been an exhausting business, and comfort food is the only thing that hits the spot. Equally, a lazy brunch while leafing through the Sunday newspapers is a wonderful restorative to body and soul. We all deserve an extra-special treat sometimes, whether a plate of pancakes or a thoroughly naughty tiramisù. And, once in a while, why shouldn't we return to the security of childhood with a plate of hearty shepherd's pie or a bowl of creamy rice pudding?

This book is divided into five chapters to make choosing your comfort dishes as easy as possible. The first offers easy-to-make midweek dishes. Many just need assembling and popping in the oven, where they will cook to perfection while you put your feet up. The second chapter provides ideas for those times when you need something heart-warming, either because the weather is cheerless or because you're feeling bleak. Filling soups, substantial stews and sticky puddings fit the bill.

Unwind at the weekend by taking your time to enjoy the recipes in the third chapter. Follow a long lie-in with a scrumptious brunch, or relax after the household chores with a long and lazy supper. The chapter of childhood favourites features all those well-loved goodies that we crave but never admit to liking in public. The final chapter offers the ultimate in comfort food — recipes all based around chocolate. Cakes, mousses, trifles and home-made fudge will take you out of this world.

You can take additional comfort from the fact that home-cooked food using fresh ingredients is the healthiest, most economical way to eat. You are, they say, what you eat, so feel comfortable in your body and enjoy some feel-good food.

comfort cooking

Some people find preparing and cooking food soothing and even therapeutic, but for others it's the end result that provides the comfort. A few helpful hints can take the pain out of preparation and put the enjoyment into eating.

Keep your storecupboard stocked up with a good supply of all the staples. Canned goods, from tomatoes to tuna, are perfect for all kinds of satisfying dishes. Canned pulses, such as beans, also help provide the basis for a flavourful meal and don't require lengthy soaking before cooking. Packs of rice, pasta and noodles provide almost-instant carbohydrate, which is in itself comfort food because it fills you up and gives you slow-release energy. Sugar, flour, cornflour, cocoa powder and dried fruit all form an excellent basis for numerous tasty treats for the sweet-toothed.

Make the most of your freezer. Not only is it worth keeping a supply of basic ingredients, such as frozen vegetables, fish and meat, you can also stock up on comfort foods that you have cooked in advance. Stews and casseroles, in particular, often taste even better after keeping than they do on the day you make them. When you're feeling energetic, cook a batch of Speedy Chilli Beef (see page 66) or Chicken, Sausage & Bean Stew (see page 42) and freeze them in individual portions for those times when you want a quick fix for

the winter blues or you feel the need for a little tender loving care. Buying some special goodies for the freezer, such as tiger prawns, when you're feeling extravagant (or it's pay day) ensures that you have the ingredients for a special treat when comfort food is the

order of the day. Don't forget that frozen pastry dough is a great stand-by for both sweet and savoury tarts and pies. Do remember to keep an eye on 'use-by' dates.

Keep kitchen equipment in good order to minimize the effort involved in preparing comfort food. Keep knives sharp to speed up slicing and chopping and reduce the risk of accidents. Good quality, heavy-based saucepans can safely be left with their contents simmering while you slip into something comfortable without the worry that supper will burn. A flameproof casserole is a doddle for one-pot dishes and reduces the washing-up – definitely a comfort factor. A reliable can opener – and, possibly, corkscrew – is a must.

Although it's always sensible to plan in advance, the recipes in this book use all kinds of meat, poultry, fish and vegetables, so you can simply buy your favourites when shopping for fresh goods. They're also very adaptable, meaning it's easy to substitute ingredients that you prefer or just happen to have at hand this particular week. If you haven't got turkey for the pie, use chicken or even pork; if you haven't got a fresh chilli, crush a dried one or use flakes.

The joy of comfort food is not simply in the eating, but in its versatility and the ease with which you can prepare and cook it.

CHAPTER I

week days:

chill out /
TV dinners

baked fish & chips

INGREDIENTS

450 g/1 lb floury potatoes, cut into thick,
even-sized chips
vegetable oil spray
55 g/2 oz plain flour
1 egg
55 g/2 oz fresh white breadcrumbs, seasoned
to taste with salt and pepper
4 cod or haddock fillets

TO GARNISH
lemon wedges
fresh parsley sprigs

SERVES 4

Preheat the oven to 200°C/400°F/Gas Mark 6. Line 2 baking sheets with non-stick liner.

Rinse the chipped potatoes under cold running water, then dry well on a clean tea towel. Put in a bowl, spray with oil and toss together until coated. Spread the chips on a baking sheet and cook in the oven for 40–45 minutes, turning once, until golden.

Meanwhile, put the flour on a plate, beat the egg in a shallow dish and spread the seasoned breadcrumbs on a large plate. Dip the fish fillets in the flour to coat, then the egg (allowing any excess to drip off) and finally the breadcrumbs, patting them firmly into the fish. Place the fish in one layer on a baking sheet.

Fifteen minutes before the chips have cooked, bake the fish fillets in the oven for 10–15 minutes, turning them once during cooking, until the fish is tender. Serve the fish with the chips, garnished with lemon wedges and parsley sprigs.

4 large baking potatoes
85 g/3 oz butter
1 large garlic clove, crushed
150 g/5¹/₂ oz mushrooms, sliced
1 tbsp snipped fresh chives
2 tbsp chopped fresh parsley
salt and pepper
175 ml/6 fl oz double cream

4 tbsp grated Cheddar cheese
4 tbsp chopped lightly toasted
   walnuts, to garnish
fresh mixed salad, to serve

jacket *potatoes* with cream *&* walnuts

SERVES 4

Preheat the oven to 190°C/375°F/Gas Mark 5. Scrub the potatoes and
pierce the skins several times with a fork. Place on a baking tray and bake
in the oven for 1¹/₄ hours, or until cooked through. About 5 minutes before
the end of the cooking time, melt 1¹/₂ tablespoons of the butter in a frying
pan over a low heat, add the garlic and mushrooms and cook, stirring, for
4 minutes, or until the mushrooms are tender. Remove from the heat and
set aside.

Remove the potatoes from the oven and cut them in half lengthways.
Carefully scoop out the potato flesh into a bowl, leaving the skins intact.
Add the remaining butter to the potato flesh, then stir in the herbs.
Season to taste with salt and pepper. Spoon the mixture into the potato
skins, then add a layer of mushrooms. Top with the cream, then the cheese.
Return the potatoes to the oven and bake for a further 10 minutes at the
same temperature. Remove from the oven, scatter over the walnuts and
serve with a mixed salad.

INGREDIENTS

2 litres/3¹/₂ pints stock or water
1 tbsp olive oil
3 tbsp butter
1 small onion, finely chopped
450 g/1 lb arborio rice
salt and pepper
55 g/2 oz freshly grated
   Parmesan cheese or Grana Padano,
   plus shavings to garnish

basic *risotto*

SERVES 4

Bring the stock to the boil, then reduce the heat and keep simmering
gently over a low heat while you are cooking the risotto. Heat the oil with
2 tablespoons of the butter in a deep saucepan over a medium heat until the
butter has melted. Stir in the onion and cook gently until soft and starting
to turn golden. Do not brown.

Add the rice and mix to coat in the oil and butter. Cook and stir for
2–3 minutes, or until the grains are translucent. Gradually add the stock,
a ladle at a time. Stir constantly and add more liquid as the rice absorbs
it. Increase the heat to moderate so that the liquid bubbles. Cook for
20 minutes, or until all the liquid is absorbed. Season to taste with salt and
pepper but don't add too much salt as the Parmesan cheese is salty. The
risotto should be of a creamy consistency with a bit of bite in the rice.

Remove the risotto from the heat and add the remaining butter. Mix well,
then stir in the Parmesan cheese until it melts. Taste and adjust the
seasoning, then serve, garnished with Parmesan cheese shavings.

pizza *dough* & pizza *topping*

INGREDIENTS

225 g/8 oz strong white bread flour,
plus extra for dusting
1 tsp easy-blend dried yeast
1 tsp salt
2 tbsp olive oil
225–350 ml/8–12 fl oz warm water

TOPPING
4 tbsp olive oil
1 large onion, thinly sliced
6 button mushrooms,
thinly sliced
1/2 small green pepper, 1/2 small red pepper
and 1/2 small yellow pepper, deseeded and
thinly sliced
300 g/10 1/2 oz ready-made
tomato pasta sauce
55 g/2 oz mozzarella cheese,
thickly sliced
2 tbsp freshly grated Parmesan cheese
1 tsp chopped fresh basil

fresh crisp salad, to serve

SERVES 2

Combine the flour, yeast and salt in a mixing bowl. Drizzle over half the oil. Make a well in the centre and pour in the water. Mix to a firm dough and shape into a ball. Turn out onto a floured work surface and knead until it is no longer sticky. Oil the bowl with the remaining oil. Put the dough in the bowl and turn to coat with oil. Cover with a tea towel and leave to rise for 1 hour.

When the dough has doubled in size, punch it down to release the excess air, then knead until smooth. Divide in half and roll into 2 thin rounds. Place on a metal tray or baking sheet.

Preheat the oven to 220°C/425°F/Gas Mark 7. For the topping, soften the vegetables for 5 minutes in the oil. Spread some of the tomato sauce over the pizza bases, but do not go right to the edge. Top with the vegetables and mozzarella cheese. Spoon over more tomato sauce, then sprinkle with Parmesan cheese and chopped basil. Bake for 10 minutes, or until the base is crispy and the cheese has melted. Serve with a crisp salad.

INGREDIENTS

6 eggs
4 tbsp milk
salt and pepper
450 g/1 lb potatoes
2 tbsp olive oil
25 g/1 oz butter
2 onions, finely chopped
1 green or red pepper, deseeded and
 finely chopped
fresh parsley sprigs, to garnish

spanish *omelette*

SERVES 4

In a bowl, beat the eggs, milk and salt and pepper to taste together. Cut the potatoes into 1-cm/^{1}/$_{2}$-inch cubes.

Heat the oil and butter in a large frying pan. Add the potatoes, onions and pepper and cook very slowly for 10–15 minutes, stirring occasionally, until almost cooked. Increase the heat and cook for a further 5–10 minutes, or until the vegetables start to brown.

Preheat the grill to high. Pour in the egg mixture and cook over a low heat for 5 minutes, or until the mixture is set and the underside is golden brown.

Transfer the pan to the grill and cook until the top is set and golden brown. Garnish the omelette with parsley sprigs and serve it hot, cut into wedges.

INGREDIENTS

1 red onion, sliced into thick rings
1 small aubergine, thickly sliced
2 large mushrooms, halved
3 red peppers, halved and deseeded
3 plum tomatoes, peeled and diced
salt and pepper
2 garlic cloves, very finely chopped
1 tbsp chopped fresh
  flat-leaf parsley
1 tsp chopped fresh rosemary

1 tsp dried thyme or oregano
finely grated rind of 1 lemon
75 g/2³/4 oz stale, coarse breadcrumbs
3 tbsp olive oil, plus extra
  for brushing
6–8 black olives, stoned and sliced
25 g/1 oz feta cheese
  (drained weight), cut into
  1-cm/¹/2-inch cubes

baked mediterranean *vegetables* with feta

SERVES 4

Preheat the grill to medium. Put the onion, aubergine, mushrooms and peppers on a large baking tray, placing the peppers cut-side down. Brush lightly with oil.

Cook under the grill for 10–12 minutes, turning the onion, aubergine and mushrooms halfway through, until beginning to blacken. Cut into even-sized chunks. Place in a shallow ovenproof dish. Arrange the diced tomatoes on top and season to taste with salt and pepper.

Preheat the oven to 220°C/425°F/Gas Mark 7.

In a bowl, combine the garlic, parsley, rosemary, thyme and lemon rind with the breadcrumbs. Season to taste with pepper. Add the oil to bind the mixture together. Scatter the mixture over the vegetables and add the olives and cheese.

Bake in the oven for 10–15 minutes, or until the vegetables are heated through and the topping is crisp. Serve straight from the dish.

mushroom &cauliflower cheese *crumble*

INGREDIENTS

salt and pepper
1 medium cauliflower
55 g/2 oz butter, plus 2 tbsp
for the topping
115 g/4 oz button mushrooms, sliced
115 g/4 oz dry breadcrumbs
2 tbsp freshly grated Parmesan cheese
1 tsp dried oregano
1 tsp dried parsley

SERVES 4

Preheat the oven to 230°C/450°F/Gas Mark 8.

Bring a large saucepan of salted water to the boil.

Break the cauliflower into small florets and cook in the boiling water for 3 minutes. Remove from the heat, drain well and transfer to a large shallow ovenproof dish.

Melt the 55 g/2 oz butter in a small frying pan over a medium heat. Add the mushrooms, stir to coat and cook gently for 3 minutes. Remove from the heat and add to the cauliflower. Season to taste with salt and pepper.

Combine the breadcrumbs, cheese and herbs in a small mixing bowl, then sprinkle the crumbs over the vegetables.

Dice the butter for the topping and dot over the crumbs.

Place the dish in the oven and bake for 15 minutes, or until the crumbs are golden brown and crisp. Serve straight from the dish.

INGREDIENTS

3 tbsp butter

1 small onion, finely chopped

6 spring onions, green part included, finely chopped

4 potatoes, cut into chunks

700 ml/1¼ pints chicken stock

salt and pepper

150 ml/5 fl oz milk

150 ml/5 fl oz whipping cream

2 tbsp chopped fresh flat-leaf parsley

75 g/2¾ oz coarsely grated Cheddar cheese

fresh flat-leaf parsley leaves, to garnish

fried garlic croûtons, to serve (optional)

creamy potato, onion *&* cheese *soup*

SERVES 4

Heat the butter in a large saucepan over a medium heat. Add the onion, spring onions and potatoes. Cover and cook for 5–7 minutes, or until the onions are just tender.

Add the stock. Bring to the boil, then cover and simmer over a medium–low heat for 15–20 minutes, or until the potatoes are tender. Remove from the heat.

Mash the potatoes and season to taste with salt and pepper. Stir in the milk, cream and chopped parsley. Reheat gently. Ladle into bowls and sprinkle with the cheese and parsley leaves.

Serve with garlic croûtons, if desired.

INGREDIENTS

salt and pepper

115 g/4 oz dried short macaroni

1 small egg, lightly beaten

2 tbsp butter

4 small leeks, green part included,
  finely sliced

2 carrots, diced

1 tbsp plain flour

1/4 tsp freshly grated nutmeg

250 ml/9 fl oz chicken stock

225 g/8 oz diced cooked turkey
  or chicken

55 g/2 oz diced ham

3 tbsp chopped fresh
  flat-leaf parsley

100 g/3 1/2 oz freshly grated
  Gruyère cheese

turkey, leek *&* cheese *gratin*

SERVES 4

Preheat the oven to 180°C/350°F/Gas Mark 4.

Cook the macaroni in plenty of boiling salted water until just tender. Drain
and return to the saucepan. Stir in the egg and a knob of the butter, mixing
well. Set aside.

Melt the remaining butter in a saucepan over a medium heat. Add the
leeks and carrots. Cover and cook for 5 minutes, shaking the saucepan
occasionally, until just tender.

Add the flour and nutmeg. Cook for 1 minute, stirring constantly. Pour in
the stock. Bring to the boil, stirring constantly. Stir in the turkey, ham and
parsley. Season to taste with salt and pepper.

Spread half the turkey mixture over the base of a shallow baking dish.
Spread the macaroni over the turkey. Top with the remaining turkey
mixture. Sprinkle with the cheese.

Bake in the oven for 15–20 minutes. Serve the gratin when the cheese is
golden and bubbling.

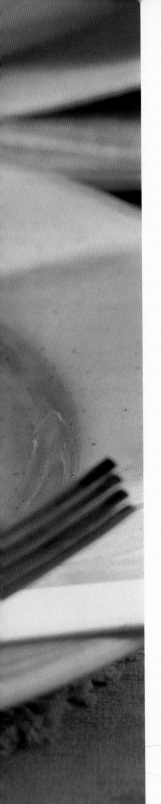

chicken & potato *pie*

INGREDIENTS

SERVES 4

PASTRY

350 g/12 oz plain flour, plus extra
for dusting
pinch of salt
175 g/6 oz butter, diced, plus extra
for greasing
about 6 tbsp cold water
milk, for brushing

FILLING

250 ml/9 fl oz chicken stock
700 g/1 lb 9 oz skinless, boneless chicken,
cut into bite-sized chunks
100 g/3½ oz potatoes, roughly chopped
1 egg, beaten
75 g/2¾ oz shelled hazelnuts,
toasted and ground
75 g/2¾ oz Cheddar cheese, grated
2 spring onions, chopped
1 tbsp chopped fresh sage
salt and pepper

selection of freshly cooked vegetables,
to serve

To make the pastry, sift the flour and salt into a bowl.
Rub in the butter until the mixture resembles breadcrumbs.
Gradually stir in enough of the cold water to make a pliable
dough. Knead lightly. Cover with clingfilm and refrigerate
for 1 hour. Meanwhile, to make the filling, bring the stock
to the boil in a saucepan. Reduce the heat, add the chicken
and potatoes and simmer for 30 minutes. Remove from the
heat, cool for 25 minutes, then drain off the liquid and
transfer the chicken and potatoes to a bowl. Stir in the
remaining filling ingredients.

Preheat the oven to 190°C/375°F/Gas Mark 5. Grease a
23-cm/9-inch pie tin. Remove the dough from the refrigerator.
On a floured work surface, shape into a ball, roll out half the
dough to a thickness of 5 mm/¼ inch and use to line the tin.
Spoon in the filling. Roll out the remaining pastry to make the
lid. Brush the pie rim with water, cover with the lid and trim
the edges. Cut 2 slits in the top. Add decorative shapes made
from the dough trimmings. Brush with milk. Bake for
45 minutes, then serve with vegetables.

INGREDIENTS

700 g/1 lb 9 oz cod fillets
600 ml/1 pint fish stock
250 g/9 oz potatoes, sliced
salt and pepper
2 tbsp butter
1 onion, sliced
1 garlic clove, chopped
1 carrot, sliced
2 celery sticks, sliced
100 g/3½ oz chestnut mushrooms, sliced

4 tomatoes, sliced
2 tbsp chopped fresh basil
1 tbsp sherry
plain flour, for dusting
1 packet frozen puff pastry, thawed
1 tbsp milk

TO SERVE
crisp lettuce leaves
freshly cooked mangetout

cod puff *pie*

SERVES 4

Preheat the oven to 200°C/400°F/Gas Mark 6. Rinse the cod and pat dry.
Bring the stock to the boil in a large saucepan, add the cod and simmer for
10 minutes. Drain, then cut into chunks. Meanwhile, cook the potatoes in
salted water for 5 minutes. Drain. Melt half the butter in a frying pan over
a low heat. Add the onion and garlic and cook for 3 minutes. Add the carrot
and celery and cook for 5 minutes. Lift out the vegetables and set aside.

Melt the remaining butter in the frying pan. Add the mushrooms and
tomatoes and cook for 7 minutes. Stir in the basil and sherry. Cook for
1 minute. On a floured work surface, roll out enough pastry to line a large
pie dish, with an overhang of 2.5 cm/1 inch. Put some of the tomato
mixture into the lined dish. Top with a layer of cod, then a vegetable layer,
then a potato layer. Repeat the layers to fill the pie. Season to taste with salt
and pepper. Top with pastry, trim and crimp, then make a slit in the top.
Decorate with fish shapes made from the dough trimmings and brush with
the milk. Bake for 30 minutes. Serve with lettuce leaves and mangetout.

INGREDIENTS

2 tbsp vegetable oil
2 tbsp butter
250 g/9 oz okra, trimmed and
  thickly sliced
1 onion, finely chopped
2 celery sticks, quartered lengthways
  and diced
1 green pepper, deseeded and diced
2 garlic cloves, very finely chopped
200 g/7 oz canned chopped tomatoes
1/2 tsp dried thyme or oregano

1 fresh bay leaf
salt and pepper
850 ml/1 1/2 pints chicken stock
  or water
450 g/1 lb fresh or frozen raw
  prawns, peeled and deveined
few drops of Tabasco sauce
2 tbsp chopped fresh coriander,
  to garnish

prawn *gumbo*

SERVES 4

Heat the oil and butter in a large saucepan over a medium heat.
Add the okra and cook, uncovered, for 15 minutes, or until it loses
its gummy consistency.

Add the onion, celery, pepper, garlic, tomatoes, thyme and bay leaf.
Season to taste with salt and pepper. Cover and cook over a medium–low
heat for 10 minutes.

Pour in the stock. Bring to the boil, then cover and simmer over a
medium–low heat for 15 minutes, or until the vegetables are al dente.
Add the prawns and Tabasco sauce. Cook for 5 minutes, or until the
prawns are pink.

Stir in the coriander to garnish just before serving.

lemon meringue *pie*

INGREDIENTS

PASTRY

200 g/7 oz plain flour, plus extra
for dusting
100 g/3¹/₂ oz butter, diced, plus extra
for greasing
50 g/1³/₄ oz icing sugar, sifted
finely grated rind of 1 lemon
1 egg yolk, beaten
3 tbsp milk

FILLING

3 tbsp cornflour
300 ml/10 fl oz cold water
juice and grated rind of 2 lemons
175 g/6 oz caster sugar
2 eggs, separated

SERVES 4

To make the pastry, sift the flour into a bowl and rub in the butter. Mix in the remaining ingredients. Knead briefly on a lightly floured work surface, then leave to rest for 30 minutes.

Preheat the oven to 180°C/350°F/Gas Mark 4. Grease a 20-cm/ 8-inch ovenproof pie dish. Roll out the pastry to a thickness of 5 mm/¹/₄ inch and use it to line the dish. Prick with a fork, line with baking paper and fill with baking beans. Bake for 15 minutes. Remove from the oven. Reduce the oven temperature to 150°C/300°F/Gas Mark 2.

To make the filling, mix the cornflour with a little water. Put the remaining water into a saucepan. Stir in the lemon juice and rind and cornflour paste. Bring to the boil, stirring. Cook for 2 minutes. Cool a little. Stir in 5 tablespoons of the caster sugar and the egg yolks, then pour the mixture into the pastry case. In a bowl, whisk the egg whites until stiff. Gradually whisk in the remaining caster sugar and spread over the pie. Bake for 40 minutes. Remove from the oven and serve.

INGREDIENTS

PASTRY
200 g/7 oz plain flour, plus extra
   for dusting
100 g/3¹/2 oz butter, diced, plus extra
   for greasing
50 g/1³/4 oz icing sugar, sifted
finely grated rind of 1 lemon
1 egg yolk, beaten
3 tbsp milk

FILLING
3 cooking apples
2 tbsp lemon juice
finely grated rind of 1 lemon
150 ml/5 fl oz clear honey
175 g/6 oz fresh white or
   wholemeal breadcrumbs
1 tsp mixed spice
pinch of freshly grated nutmeg

whipped cream, to serve

spiced apple *tart*

SERVES 4

To make the pastry, sift the flour into a bowl and rub in the butter. Mix in
the remaining ingredients. Knead briefly on a lightly floured work surface,
then leave to rest for 30 minutes.

Preheat the oven to 200°C/400°F/Gas Mark 6. Grease a 20-cm/8-inch
flan tin. Roll out the pastry to a thickness of 5 mm/¹/4 inch and use to line
the base and sides of the tin.

To make the filling, core 2 of the apples and grate them into a bowl.
Add half the lemon juice and all the lemon rind, along with the honey,
breadcrumbs and mixed spice. Mix together well. Spoon evenly into the
pastry case. Core and slice the remaining apple and use to decorate the top
of the tart. Brush the apple slices with the remaining lemon juice, then
sprinkle over the nutmeg. Bake in the oven for 35 minutes, or until firm.
Remove from the oven and serve with whipped cream.

INGREDIENTS

250 g/9 oz blueberries
250 g/9 oz raspberries
250 g/9 oz blackberries
100 g/3¹/₂ oz caster sugar
200 g/7 oz plain flour, plus extra
  for dusting
25 g/1 oz ground hazelnuts
100 g/3¹/₂ oz butter, diced, plus extra
  for greasing

finely grated rind of 1 lemon
1 egg yolk, beaten
4 tbsp milk
2 tsp icing sugar, for dusting
whipped cream, to serve

forest fruit *pie*

SERVES 4

Put the fruit into a saucepan with 3 tablespoons of the caster sugar and
simmer, stirring, for 5 minutes. Remove from the heat. Sift the flour into a
bowl, then add the hazelnuts. Rub in the butter, then sift in the remaining
caster sugar. Add the lemon rind, egg yolk and 3 tablespoons of the milk
and mix. Knead briefly on a lightly floured work surface, then leave to rest
for 30 minutes.

Preheat the oven to 190°C/375°F/Gas Mark 5. Grease a 20-cm/8-inch
ovenproof pie dish. Roll out half the pastry to a thickness of 5 mm/¹/₄ inch
and use to line the dish. Spoon the fruit into the pastry case. Brush the rim
with water, then roll out the remaining dough and use it to cover the pie.
Trim and crimp round the edges, make 2 small slits in the top and decorate
with 2 leaf shapes cut from the dough trimmings. Brush all over with the
remaining milk. Bake for 40 minutes. Remove from the oven, sprinkle over
the icing sugar and serve with whipped cream.

apricot *crumble*

INGREDIENTS

125 g/4¹/2 oz butter, plus extra
for greasing
175 g/6 oz soft light brown sugar
500 g/1 lb 2 oz fresh apricots, stoned and
sliced
1 tsp ground cinnamon
175 g/6 oz plain wholemeal flour
50 g/1³/4 oz shelled hazelnuts, toasted and
finely chopped
clotted cream, to serve

SERVES 4

Preheat the oven to 200°C/400°F/Gas Mark 6. Grease a 1.2-litre/
2-pint ovenproof dish.

Put 3 tablespoons of the butter and 100 g/3¹/2 oz of the sugar into
a saucepan and melt together, stirring, over a low heat. Add the
apricots and cinnamon, cover and simmer for 5 minutes.

Meanwhile, put the flour into a bowl and rub in the remaining
butter. Stir in the remaining sugar, then the hazelnuts. Remove
the fruit from the heat and arrange in the bottom of the prepared
dish. Sprinkle the crumble topping evenly over the fruit until it
is covered all over. Transfer to the oven and bake for 25 minutes,
or until the topping is golden. Remove from the oven and serve
with clotted cream.

CHAPTER 2

rainy days:

blues

chasers

scotch *broth*

INGREDIENTS

1 large onion, quartered
6 lamb shanks, weighing about
1.6 kg/3 lb 8 oz
1 whole garlic bulb, unpeeled,
the outer loose layers removed
4 unsmoked bacon rashers, diced
1 tbsp vegetable oil
1 large onion, diced
3 carrots, sliced
1 small swede, cut into chunks
1 small celeriac, cut into chunks
3 leeks, halved lengthways and
thickly sliced
3 fresh thyme sprigs
1 fresh bay leaf
1 tsp salt
1 tsp pepper
850 ml/1½ pints chicken or beef stock
55 g/2 oz pearl barley
4 tbsp chopped fresh parsley

SERVES 6

Preheat the oven to 230°C/450°F/Gas Mark 8. Roast the quartered onion, lamb and garlic in a roasting tin for 30 minutes, or until well browned, turning occasionally. Turn into a large heavy saucepan. Pour over water to cover. Slowly bring to the boil, skimming off any foam. Cook over a low heat, partially covered, for 1¼ hours.

Meanwhile, crisp the bacon in the oil in a separate large saucepan. Add the diced onion, vegetables, herbs, salt and pepper. Pour over the stock and add the barley. Bring to the boil, then reduce the heat, cover and simmer for 35–40 minutes.

Remove the lamb and garlic from the first saucepan with a slotted spoon. Strip the meat from the bones and squeeze out the garlic pulp. Line a sieve with kitchen paper. Strain the lamb cooking liquid into a bowl. Blot up any surface fat with kitchen paper. Add 700 ml/1¼ pints of the strained liquid, with the meat and garlic pulp, to the vegetables in the other saucepan. Bring to the boil, then simmer for 10 minutes.

Stir in the parsley just before serving.

INGREDIENTS

225 g/8 oz red split lentils
1.5 litres/2³/4 pints vegetable stock
1 garlic clove, chopped
1 onion, chopped
1 leek, chopped
1 large carrot, chopped
5 tomatoes, peeled and chopped
1 bay leaf
salt and pepper
175 g/6 oz potatoes, chopped

75 g/2³/4 oz sweet potato, chopped
150 g/5¹/2 oz smoked ham, diced
pinch of freshly grated nutmeg

TO GARNISH
4 tbsp soured cream
paprika

fresh crusty bread, to serve

ham & lentil *soup*

SERVES 4

Put the lentils into a large saucepan, pour in the stock and leave to soak
for 2 hours. Add the garlic, onion, leek, carrot, tomatoes and bay leaf and
season to taste with salt and pepper. Bring to the boil, then reduce the heat,
cover and simmer for 1 hour, stirring occasionally.

Add all the potatoes with the ham, re-cover and simmer for a further
25 minutes, or until the potatoes are tender.

Remove and discard the bay leaf. Transfer half the soup to a food processor
and process for 1 minute, or until smooth. Return the mixture to the
saucepan containing the rest of the soup, add the nutmeg and adjust the
seasoning to taste, then re-heat gently until warmed through. Ladle into
bowls, garnish with a spoonful of soured cream and sprinkle over a little
paprika. Serve with fresh crusty bread.

INGREDIENTS

2 tbsp olive oil
1 onion, chopped
1 garlic clove, chopped
1 tbsp chopped fresh root ginger
1 small fresh red chilli, deseeded and
  finely chopped
2 tbsp chopped fresh coriander
1 bay leaf

1 kg/2 lb 4 oz pumpkin, deseeded
  and diced
600 ml/1 pint vegetable stock
salt and pepper
single cream, to garnish

spiced pumpkin *soup*

SERVES 4

Heat the oil in a saucepan over a medium heat. Add the onion and
garlic and cook, stirring, for 4 minutes, or until slightly softened. Add the
ginger, chilli, coriander, bay leaf and pumpkin and cook for a further
3 minutes.

Pour in the stock and bring to the boil. Using a slotted spoon, skim any
scum from the surface. Reduce the heat and simmer gently, stirring
occasionally, for 25 minutes, or until the pumpkin is tender. Remove from
the heat, discard the bay leaf and leave to cool a little.

Transfer the soup to a food processor and blend until smooth (you may
have to do this in batches). Return the soup to the saucepan and season to
taste with salt and pepper. Re-heat gently, stirring. Remove from the heat
and pour into 4 warmed soup bowls. Garnish each one with a swirl of
cream and serve.

winter *minestrone* with sausage

INGREDIENTS

3 tbsp olive oil
250 g/9 oz coarse-textured pork sausage, skinned and cut into chunks
1 onion, thinly sliced
2 garlic cloves, very finely chopped
200 g/7 oz canned chopped tomatoes
2 tbsp chopped fresh mixed herbs, such as flat-leaf parsley, sage and marjoram
1 celery stick, thinly sliced
1 carrot, diced
1 small red pepper, deseeded and diced
850 ml/1½ pints chicken stock
salt and pepper
50 g/1¾ oz dried short macaroni
75 g/2¾ oz canned, drained haricot beans
115 g/4 oz frozen peas
2 tbsp freshly grated Parmesan cheese, plus extra to serve
4 thick slices ciabatta or French bread, to serve

SERVES 4

Heat the oil in a large saucepan over a medium–low heat. Add the sausage and onion and cook, stirring occasionally, until the onion is just coloured.

Add the garlic, tomatoes and herbs and cook for 5 minutes, stirring. Add the celery, carrot and pepper, cover and cook for 5 minutes.

Pour in the stock. Bring to the boil, then reduce the heat, cover and simmer gently for 30 minutes.

Season to taste with salt and pepper. Add the macaroni and beans and simmer for 15 minutes, or until the macaroni is just tender.

Stir in the peas and cook for a further 5 minutes. Stir in the Parmesan cheese.

To serve, place the bread in individual serving bowls. Ladle the soup over the bread and leave to stand for a few minutes. Serve with plenty of extra Parmesan cheese.

450 g/1 lb potatoes
2 tbsp sunflower oil
salt and pepper

home-made oven *chips*

SERVES 4

Preheat the oven to 200°C/400°F/Gas Mark 6.

Cut the potatoes into thick, even-sized chips. Rinse them under cold running water and then dry well on a clean tea towel. Put in a bowl, add the oil and toss together until coated.

Spread the chips on a baking sheet and cook in the oven for 40–45 minutes, turning once, until golden. Add salt and pepper to taste and serve hot.

INGREDIENTS

2 whole garlic bulbs
1 tbsp olive oil
900 g/2 lb floury potatoes
salt and pepper
125 ml/4 fl oz milk
55 g/2 oz butter
fresh parsley sprigs, to garnish

roasted garlic mashed *potatoes*

SERVES 4

Preheat the oven to 180°C/350°F/Gas Mark 4.

Separate the garlic cloves but do not peel, place on a large piece of foil and
drizzle with the oil. Wrap the garlic in the foil and roast in the oven for
1 hour, or until very tender. Leave to cool slightly.

Twenty minutes before the end of the cooking time, cut the potatoes
into chunks, then cook in a saucepan of lightly salted water for 15 minutes,
or until tender.

Meanwhile, squeeze the cooled garlic cloves out of their skins and push
through a sieve into a separate saucepan. Add the milk and butter. Season
to taste with salt and pepper and heat gently until the butter has melted.

Drain the cooked potatoes, then mash in the saucepan until smooth. Pour
in the garlic mixture and heat gently, stirring, until the ingredients are
combined. Garnish with parsley sprigs and serve hot.

INGREDIENTS

2 tbsp vegetable oil

4 skinless, boneless chicken breasts,
  cubed

225 g/8 oz coarse-textured pork
  sausage, cut into large chunks

4 frankfurter sausages, halved

1 onion, finely chopped

3 carrots, finely sliced

1 garlic clove, very finely chopped

1 tsp dried thyme

$^1/_4$–$^1/_2$ tsp dried chilli flakes

400 g/14 oz canned chopped tomatoes

400 g/14 oz canned cannellini beans,
  drained and rinsed

150 ml/5 fl oz chicken stock

salt and pepper

chopped fresh flat-leaf parsley,
  to garnish

chicken, sausage & bean *stew*

SERVES 4

Heat the oil in a large heavy-based saucepan over a medium–high
heat. Cook the chicken, sausage and frankfurters until lightly browned.
Reduce the heat to medium. Add the onion and carrots and cook for
5 minutes, or until soft.

Stir in the garlic, thyme and chilli flakes. Cook for 1 minute. Add
the tomatoes, beans and stock and season to taste with salt and pepper.
Bring to the boil, then simmer over a low heat for 20–30 minutes,
stirring occasionally.

Garnish with parsley just before serving.

INGREDIENTS

2 tbsp olive oil

175 g/6 oz piece unsmoked bacon,
  sliced into thin strips

1.3 kg/3 lb stewing beef, cut into
  5-cm/2-inch pieces

2 carrots, sliced

2 onions, chopped

2 garlic cloves, very finely chopped

3 tbsp plain flour

700 ml/1¼ pints red wine

350–450 ml/12–16 fl oz beef stock

bouquet garni sachet

1 tsp salt

½ tsp pepper

3 tbsp butter

350 g/12 oz pickling onions

350 g/12 oz button mushrooms

2 tbsp chopped fresh parsley

beef *bourguignon*

SERVES 6

Heat the oil in a large flameproof casserole, add the bacon and lightly
brown. Remove with a slotted spoon. Brown the beef, in batches, in the
casserole, drain and set aside with the bacon. Add the carrots and chopped
onions to the casserole and cook for 5 minutes, or until softened. Add the
garlic and cook until just coloured. Return the meat and bacon to the
casserole. Sprinkle over the flour and cook for 1 minute, stirring. Add the
wine and enough stock to cover, the bouquet garni, salt and pepper. Bring
to the boil, then reduce the heat, cover and simmer gently for 3 hours.

Heat half the butter in a frying pan. Add the pickling onions, cover and cook
until soft. Remove with a slotted spoon and keep warm. Add the remaining
butter to the pan and cook the mushrooms. Remove and keep warm.

Strain the casserole liquid into a saucepan. Wipe the casserole and tip in the
meat, bacon, mushrooms and onions. Remove the surface fat from the
cooking liquid and simmer for 1–2 minutes to reduce. Pour over the meat
and vegetables. Serve sprinkled with parsley.

beef pot *roast* with potatoes *&* dill

INGREDIENTS

SERVES 6

2¹/₂ tbsp plain flour
1 tsp salt
¹/₄ tsp pepper
1.6 kg/3 lb 8 oz rolled brisket
2 tbsp vegetable oil
2 tbsp butter
1 onion, finely chopped
2 celery sticks, diced
2 carrots, diced
1 tsp dill seed
1 tsp dried thyme or oregano
350 ml/12 fl oz red wine
150–225 ml/5–8 fl oz beef stock
4–5 potatoes, cut into large chunks and
boiled until just tender
fresh dill sprigs, to serve

Preheat the oven to 140°C/275°F/Gas Mark 1. Mix 2 tablespoons of the flour with the salt and pepper in a shallow dish. Dip the meat in the seasoned flour to coat. Heat the oil in a flameproof casserole and brown the meat all over. Transfer to a plate. Heat half the butter in the casserole, add the onion, celery, carrots, dill seed and thyme and cook for 5 minutes. Return the meat and juices to the casserole.

Pour in the wine and enough stock to reach one-third of the way up the meat. Bring to the boil and cover. Transfer to the oven and cook for 3 hours, turning every 30 minutes. After 2 hours, add the potatoes and more stock if needed.

When ready, transfer the meat and vegetables to a warmed serving dish. Strain the cooking liquid into a saucepan.

Mix the remaining butter and flour to a paste. Bring the cooking liquid to the boil. Whisk in small pieces of the flour/butter paste, continuing to whisk until the sauce is smooth. Pour the sauce over the meat and vegetables. Sprinkle with dill sprigs and serve.

INGREDIENTS

225 g/8 oz dried chickpeas, soaked

3 tbsp vegetable oil

$^1/_2$ tsp cumin seeds

$^1/_2$ tsp mustard seeds

1 onion, finely chopped

2 garlic cloves, very finely chopped

2-cm/$^3/_4$-inch piece fresh root ginger, very finely chopped

1 tsp salt

2 tsp ground coriander

1 tsp turmeric

$^1/_2$ tsp cayenne pepper

2 tbsp tomato purée

400 g/14 oz canned chopped tomatoes

2 potatoes, cubed

3 tbsp chopped fresh coriander

1 tbsp lemon juice

250–300 ml/9–10 fl oz chicken or vegetable stock

thinly sliced white or red onion rings, to garnish

freshly cooked rice, to serve

chickpea & potato *curry*

SERVES 6

Boil the chickpeas rapidly in plenty of water for 15 minutes. Reduce the heat and boil gently for 1 hour, or until tender. Drain and set aside.

Heat the oil in a large saucepan or high-sided frying pan. Stirring all the time, add the cumin and mustard seeds, cover and cook for a few seconds, or until the seeds pop. Add the onion, cover and cook for 3–5 minutes, or until just brown. Add the garlic and ginger and cook for a few seconds. Stir in the salt, ground coriander, turmeric and cayenne, then the tomato purée and tomatoes. Simmer for a few minutes. Add the chickpeas, potatoes and 2 tablespoons of the fresh coriander.

Stir in the lemon juice and 250 ml/9 fl oz of the stock. Bring to the boil, then reduce the heat, cover and simmer for 30–40 minutes, or until the potatoes are cooked. Add the extra stock if the mixture becomes too dry.

Serve on a bed of rice, garnished with onion rings and the remaining fresh coriander.

INGREDIENTS

120 g/4¼ oz butter, softened, plus
  extra for greasing
120 g/4¼ oz soft light brown sugar
2 eggs
75 g/2¾ oz plain flour
½ tsp baking powder
2 tbsp unsweetened cocoa powder
150 g/5½ oz blueberries, plus extra
  to decorate

RUM SYRUP

120 g/4¼ oz plain dark chocolate,
  chopped
2 tbsp maple syrup
1 tbsp unsalted butter
1 tbsp rum

blueberry *chocolate pudding* with rum syrup

SERVES 4

Grease a large pudding basin. Heat water to a depth of 7.5–10 cm/
3–4 inches in a large saucepan over a low heat until simmering.

Put the butter, sugar, eggs, flour, baking powder and cocoa powder
into a large bowl and beat together until thoroughly mixed. Stir in
the blueberries. Spoon the mixture into the prepared basin and cover
tightly with 2 layers of foil. Carefully place the basin in the saucepan
of simmering water, ensuring that the water level is comfortably lower
than the basin's rim. Steam the pudding for 1 hour, topping up with boiling
water when necessary.

About 5 minutes before the end of the cooking time, heat the ingredients
for the rum syrup in a small saucepan over a low heat, stirring, until
smooth and melted. Remove the pudding from the heat, discard the foil
and run a knife around the edge to loosen the pudding. Turn out on to
a serving dish, pour over the syrup and decorate with blueberries.
Serve immediately.

jam *roly poly*

INGREDIENTS

175 g/6 oz self-raising flour, plus extra
for dusting
pinch of salt
75 g/2³/₄ oz shredded suet
3–4 tbsp hot water
6 tbsp raspberry jam
2 tbsp milk
1 tbsp butter, for greasing
fresh raspberries, to decorate
hot custard, to serve

SERVES 4

Put the flour and salt into a bowl and mix together well. Add the suet, then stir in enough of the hot water to make a light dough. Using your hands, shape the dough into a ball. Turn out the dough on to a lightly floured work surface and knead gently until smooth. Roll out into a rectangle about 28 x 23 cm/ 11 x 9 inches.

Spread the jam over the dough, leaving a border of about 1 cm/ ¹/₂ inch all round. Brush the border with milk. Starting with the short side, roll up the dough evenly until you have one large roll.

Lightly grease a large piece of foil, then place the dough roll in the centre. Gently close up the foil around the dough, allowing room for expansion, and seal tightly. Transfer to a steamer set over a saucepan of boiling water. Steam for 1¹/₂ hours, or until cooked, topping up with boiling water when necessary.

Turn out the roly poly on to a serving platter and decorate with raspberries. Serve with hot custard.

1 tbsp butter, for greasing
85 g/3 oz sultanas
5 tbsp caster sugar
90 g/3¹/₄ oz pudding rice
1.2 litres/2 pints milk
1 tsp vanilla essence
finely grated rind of 1 large lemon
pinch of freshly grated nutmeg
chopped pistachio nuts, to decorate

creamy rice *pudding*

SERVES 4

Preheat the oven to 160°C/325°F/Gas Mark 3. Grease an 850-ml/
1¹/₂-pint ovenproof dish with butter.

Put the sultanas, sugar and rice into a mixing bowl, then stir in the milk
and vanilla essence. Transfer to the prepared dish, sprinkle over the lemon
rind and the nutmeg, then bake in the oven for 2¹/₂ hours.

Remove from the oven and transfer to individual serving bowls. Decorate
with chopped pistachio nuts and serve.

INGREDIENTS

PUDDING
75 g/2³/4 oz sultanas
150 g/5¹/2 oz stoned dates, chopped
1 tsp bicarbonate of soda
2 tbsp butter, plus extra for greasing
200 g/7 oz soft light brown sugar
2 eggs
200 g/7 oz self-raising flour, sifted

STICKY TOFFEE SAUCE
2 tbsp butter
175 ml/6 fl oz double cream
200 g/7 oz soft light brown sugar
thin strips of orange zest, to decorate
whipped cream, to serve

sticky toffee *pudding*

SERVES 4

Preheat the oven to 180°C/350°F/Gas Mark 4. Grease a 20-cm/8-inch round cake tin.

To make the pudding, put the fruit and bicarbonate of soda into a heatproof bowl. Cover with boiling water and leave to soak. Put the butter in a separate bowl, add the sugar and mix well. Beat in the eggs, then fold in the flour. Drain the soaked fruit, add to the bowl and mix. Spoon the mixture evenly into the prepared cake tin. Transfer to the oven and bake for 35–40 minutes. The pudding is cooked when a skewer inserted into the centre comes out clean.

About 5 minutes before the end of the cooking time, make the sauce. Melt the butter in a saucepan over a medium heat. Stir in the cream and sugar and bring to the boil, stirring constantly. Reduce the heat and simmer for 5 minutes.

Turn out the pudding on to a serving plate and pour over the sauce. Decorate with strips of orange zest and serve with whipped cream.

CHAPTER 3

lazy

weekends

900 g/2 lb floury potatoes
salt and pepper
4 skinless, boneless chicken breasts
2 tbsp vegetable oil
1 onion, finely chopped
1 garlic clove, finely chopped
2 tbsp chopped fresh parsley
4 eggs

chicken *hash* with fried *eggs*

SERVES 4

Cut the potatoes into 2-cm/3/4-inch dice and cook in a large saucepan of lightly salted water for 5 minutes, or until just tender. Drain well.

Cut the chicken into 2-cm/3/4-inch pieces. Heat half the oil in a large frying pan. Add the onion and garlic and cook, stirring, for 5 minutes, or until the onion has softened. Add the chicken and season to taste with salt and pepper. Cook, stirring, for a further 5 minutes, or until the onion and chicken have browned.

Add the drained potatoes and cook, stirring occasionally, for 10 minutes, or until the potatoes have browned. Stir in the parsley.

Meanwhile, in a separate frying pan, heat the remaining oil. Break the eggs individually into the hot oil and cook until set.

Divide the chicken hash between individual serving plates and top each serving with a fried egg.

INGREDIENTS

450 g/1 lb potatoes
1 egg, beaten
4 tbsp plain flour, plus extra
  for dusting
salt and pepper
450 g/1 lb sliced lambs' liver
sunflower oil, for frying
4 bacon rashers
2 onions, finely sliced
fresh parsley sprigs, to garnish

pan-fried liver *&* bacon with potato *cakes*

SERVES 4

Grate the potatoes, then rinse under cold running water until the water runs clear. Squeeze out the water and dry the potatoes in a clean tea towel. Put the potatoes into a large bowl and add the egg and flour, then season to taste with salt and pepper and mix well together.

Dust the liver with flour and season to taste with salt and pepper.

Heat about 5 mm/¼ inch oil in a large frying pan, then add large tablespoons of the potato mixture, flattening them with a spatula. Cook, turning once, for 10 minutes, or until golden brown. Remove from the pan and keep hot. Continue until all the mixture has been cooked.

Meanwhile, in a separate frying pan, heat enough oil to cover the base. Add the bacon and cook until crisp, then push to one side of the pan. Add the onions and cook for 5 minutes, or until browned. Push to one side of the pan, add the liver and cook, turning once, for 6–8 minutes, or until tender. Serve with the potato cakes, garnished with parsley sprigs.

salisbury *steak*

INGREDIENTS

1 tbsp vegetable oil
1 small onion, thinly sliced
4 button mushrooms, thinly sliced
115 g/4 oz fresh beef mince
salt and pepper
1/4 ciabatta loaf
1 tomato, sliced (optional)
50 ml/2 fl oz red wine or beef stock

SERVES I

Heat the oil in a small frying pan over a high heat. Add the onion and mushrooms and cook quickly until soft. Push the vegetables to the side of the pan.

Season the beef to taste with salt and pepper, then shape into a round patty. Add to the frying pan and cook until starting to brown, then carefully flip over and cook the second side.

Slice the ciabatta horizontally through the centre, toast lightly and arrange on a serving dish. Top with the tomato slices, if using.

Remove the meat patty from the pan and set it on the ciabatta.

Bring the onions and mushrooms back to the centre of the pan, pour over the wine and heat until boiling. Continue boiling for 1 minute, or until slightly reduced, then remove from the heat and spoon over the meat patty. Serve immediately.

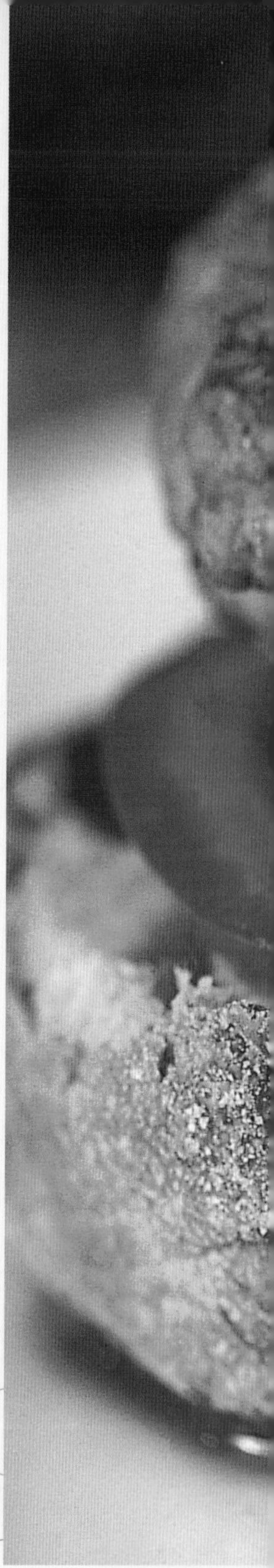

INGREDIENTS

450 g/1 lb frozen spinach, thawed
salt and pepper
450 g/1 lb ricotta cheese
8 sheets no-precook lasagne
500 ml/18 fl oz passata
225 g/8 oz mozzarella cheese,
  thinly sliced
1 tbsp freshly grated Parmesan cheese
fresh salad, to serve (optional)

cheese & spinach *lasagne*

SERVES 4

Preheat the oven to 180°C/350°F/Gas Mark 4.

Put the spinach in a sieve and squeeze out any excess liquid. Put half in the bottom of an ovenproof dish and season to taste with salt and pepper.

Spread half the ricotta over the spinach, cover with half the lasagne sheets, then spoon over half the passata. Arrange half the mozzarella cheese slices on top. Repeat the layers and finally sprinkle over the Parmesan cheese.

Bake in the oven for 45–50 minutes, or until the top is brown and bubbling.

Serve with salad, if desired.

INGREDIENTS

350 g/12 oz haddock fillets
350 g/12 oz halibut fillets
350 g/12 oz salmon fillets
600 ml/1 pint milk
125 ml/4 fl oz brandy
1 kg/2 lb 4 oz potatoes, sliced
salt and pepper
5 tbsp butter, plus extra for greasing

3 tbsp plain flour
1 tbsp chopped fresh parsley
1 tbsp chopped fresh coriander
2 onions, 1 grated and 1 sliced
85 g/3 oz Cheddar cheese, grated
selection of freshly cooked
　vegetables, to serve

mixed fish & potato *pie*

SERVES 4

Preheat the oven to 200°C/400°F/Gas Mark 6. Rinse all the fish, then pat
dry with kitchen paper. Pour the milk into a saucepan and bring to the
boil. Add the haddock and halibut and cook gently for 10 minutes. Lift out
and set aside. Reserve the milk. In a separate saucepan, cook the salmon in
the brandy over a low heat for 10 minutes. Lift out and set aside. Reserve
the cooking liquid. Cut all the fish into small chunks.

Cook the potatoes in a large saucepan of lightly salted water for 15 minutes.
Meanwhile, in a separate small saucepan, melt the butter over a low heat,
stir in the flour and cook for 1 minute. Stir in the reserved milk and brandy
liquid to make a smooth sauce. Bring to the boil, then reduce the heat and
simmer for 10 minutes. Remove from the heat and stir in the herbs. Drain
and mash the potatoes, then add the grated onion. Season to taste with salt
and pepper. Grease a large pie dish, then add the fish. Top with the sliced
onion. Pour over enough sauce to cover. Top with the mashed potato, then
the cheese. Bake for 30 minutes. Serve with vegetables.

moussaka

INGREDIENTS

2 aubergines, thinly sliced
450 g/1 lb fresh lean beef mince
2 onions, finely sliced
1 tsp finely chopped garlic
400 g/14 oz canned tomatoes
2 tbsp chopped fresh parsley
salt and pepper
2 eggs
300 ml/10 fl oz low-fat
natural yogurt
1 tbsp freshly grated Parmesan cheese

SERVES 4

In a large non-stick frying pan, dry-fry the aubergine slices, in batches, on both sides until brown. Remove from the pan.

Add the beef to the pan and cook for 5 minutes, stirring, until browned. Stir in the onions and garlic and cook for 5 minutes, or until lightly browned. Add the tomatoes and parsley and season to taste with salt and pepper. Bring the mixture to the boil, then reduce the heat and simmer for 20 minutes, or until the meat is tender.

Preheat the oven to 180°C/350°F/Gas Mark 4. Arrange half the aubergine slices in a layer in an ovenproof dish. Add the meat mixture, then a final layer of the remaining aubergine slices.

In a bowl, beat the eggs, then beat in the yogurt and add salt and pepper to taste. Pour the mixture over the aubergine and sprinkle the cheese on top. Bake the moussaka in the oven for 45 minutes, or until golden brown. Serve straight from the dish.

INGREDIENTS

2 tbsp olive oil

225 g/8 oz coarse-textured pure
  pork sausage, skinned and cut
  into chunks

2 onions, finely chopped

4 carrots, thickly sliced

6 potatoes, cut into chunks

2 large garlic cloves,
  very finely chopped

2 tsp chopped fresh rosemary

2 tsp chopped fresh thyme or oregano

1.2 kg/2 lb 10 oz canned
  chopped tomatoes

salt and pepper

2 tbsp chopped fresh flat-leaf
  parsley, to garnish

sausage & tomato *hotpot*

SERVES 4

Heat the oil in a large heavy-based saucepan over a medium–high heat.
Add the sausage and cook until browned. Remove from the saucepan with
a slotted spoon and set aside.

Reduce the heat to medium. Add the onions, carrots, potatoes, garlic,
rosemary and thyme to the saucepan. Cover and cook gently for
10 minutes, stirring occasionally.

Return the sausage to the saucepan. Pour in the tomatoes and bring to
the boil. Season to taste with salt and pepper. Cover and simmer over a
medium–low heat, stirring occasionally, for 45 minutes, or until the
vegetables are tender.

Sprinkle with the parsley just before serving.

INGREDIENTS

2 tbsp vegetable oil

450 g/1 lb skinless, boneless
   chicken breasts, cubed

1 onion, finely chopped

1 green pepper, deseeded and
   finely chopped

1 potato, diced

1 sweet potato, diced

2 garlic cloves, very finely chopped

1–2 fresh green chillies, deseeded and
   very finely chopped

200 g/7 oz canned chopped tomatoes

$^{1}/_{2}$ tsp dried oregano

$^{1}/_{2}$ tsp salt

$^{1}/_{4}$ tsp pepper

4 tbsp chopped fresh coriander

450 ml/16 fl oz chicken stock

mexican chicken, *chilli* & potato *pot*

SERVES 4

Heat the oil in a large heavy-based saucepan over a medium–high heat.
Add the chicken and cook until lightly browned.

Reduce the heat to medium. Add the onion, pepper, potato and sweet
potato. Cover and cook, stirring occasionally, for 5 minutes, or until the
vegetables begin to soften.

Add the garlic and chillies and cook for 1 minute. Stir in the tomatoes,
oregano, salt, pepper and half the coriander and cook for 1 minute.

Pour in the stock. Bring to the boil, then cover and simmer over a
medium–low heat for 15–20 minutes, or until the chicken is cooked
through and the vegetables are tender.

Sprinkle with the remaining coriander just before serving.

lamb, garlic & bean *casserole*

INGREDIENTS

2 tbsp olive oil, plus extra for drizzling
900 g/2 lb boneless lamb, cut into
4-cm/1¹/₂-inch cubes
2 onions, finely chopped
1 tbsp chopped fresh rosemary
12 large garlic cloves, peeled and left whole
2–3 anchovy fillets, roughly chopped
2 tbsp plain flour
¹/₂ tsp pepper
600 ml/1 pint chicken or lamb stock
225 g/8 oz dried cannellini or haricot beans,
soaked overnight and drained
salt
115 g/4 oz stale, coarse breadcrumbs
chopped fresh flat-leaf parsley,
to garnish

SERVES 4

Preheat the oven to 150°C/300°F/Gas Mark 2. Heat half the oil in a flameproof casserole. When very hot, cook the lamb, in batches, until evenly browned. Remove with a slotted spoon and transfer to a plate. Cook the onions and rosemary in the remaining oil in the casserole, stirring, for 5–7 minutes, or until golden brown. Reduce the heat, stir in the garlic and anchovies and cook for 1 minute.

Return the meat and any juices to the casserole. Sprinkle with the flour and stir well. Season with the pepper. Pour in the stock, stirring constantly, and add the drained beans.

Bring to the boil, cover tightly and cook in the oven for 2 hours, or until soft. Remove from the oven. Season to taste with salt.

Preheat the grill to high. Spread the breadcrumbs over the lamb and beans. Drizzle a little oil over the top. Place under the grill for a few minutes, or until the crumbs are golden brown. Sprinkle with parsley and serve immediately.

INGREDIENTS

3 tbsp vegetable oil
450 g/1 lb fresh beef mince
1 onion, finely chopped
1 green pepper, deseeded and diced
2 garlic cloves, very finely chopped
800 g/1 lb 12 oz canned
  chopped tomatoes
400 g/14 oz canned red kidney beans,
  drained and rinsed
1 tsp ground cumin

1 tsp salt
1 tsp sugar
1–3 tsp chilli powder
2 tbsp chopped fresh coriander

speedy *chilli* beef

SERVES 4

Heat the oil in a large flameproof casserole over a medium–high heat. Add the beef and cook, stirring, until lightly browned.

Reduce the heat to medium. Add the onion, pepper and garlic and cook for 5 minutes, or until soft.

Stir in the remaining ingredients, except the coriander. Bring to the boil, then simmer over a medium–low heat, stirring frequently, for 30 minutes.

Stir in the coriander just before serving.

INGREDIENTS

4 tbsp plain flour

salt and pepper

50 ml/2 fl oz olive oil

8 pieces neck of lamb or lamb cutlets

1 green pepper, deseeded and
  thinly sliced

1–2 fresh green chillies,
  deseeded and thinly sliced

1 small onion, thinly sliced

2 garlic cloves, thinly sliced

2 tbsp fresh basil, roughly torn

125 ml/4 fl oz red wine

4 tbsp red wine vinegar

8 cherry tomatoes

125 ml/4 fl oz water

1 quantity Basic Risotto
  (see page 13), made with
  beef stock and red wine

hot pepper lamb in red wine *risotto*

SERVES 4

Mix the flour with salt and pepper to taste on a plate. Heat the oil in a frying pan large enough to take all the lamb in a single layer over a high heat. Dredge the lamb in the seasoned flour, shaking off any excess. Brown the lamb in the pan, remove with a slotted spoon and set aside.

Toss the pepper, chillies, onion, garlic and basil in the oil left in the pan for 3 minutes, or until lightly browned. Add the wine and vinegar, bring to the boil and continue cooking over a high heat for 3–4 minutes, or until reduced to 2 tablespoons.

Add the tomatoes and water to the pan, stir and bring to the boil. Return the meat, cover and reduce the heat as low as possible. Cook for 30 minutes, or until the meat is tender, turning occasionally. Check regularly and add 2–3 tablespoons of water if necessary. Meanwhile, prepare the Basic Risotto as on page 13. Arrange a scoop of risotto on each plate and sprinkle with some peppers and tomatoes. Arrange the lamb on top and serve.

baked pears with chocolate *custard*

INGREDIENTS

4 ripe pears
1 tbsp lime juice
2 tbsp red wine
55 g/2 oz butter
4 tbsp soft light brown sugar
1 tsp mixed spice

CHOCOLATE CUSTARD
1 heaped tbsp custard powder
1 tbsp cornflour
1 tbsp unsweetened cocoa powder
1 tbsp soft light brown sugar
250 ml/9 fl oz milk
350 ml/12 fl oz single cream
2 tbsp grated plain dark chocolate

thin strips of lime zest, to decorate

SERVES 4

Preheat the oven to 200°C/400°F/Gas Mark 6. Peel and core the pears, leaving them whole, then brush with lime juice. Put the pears into a small, non-stick baking tin, then pour over the wine.

Heat the butter, sugar and mixed spice in a small saucepan over a low heat, stirring, until melted. Pour the mixture over the pears. Bake in the oven, basting occasionally, for 25 minutes, or until golden and cooked through.

About 5 minutes before the end of the cooking time, heat the custard powder, cornflour, cocoa powder, sugar and milk in a saucepan over a low heat, stirring, until thickened and almost boiling. Remove from the heat, add the cream and grated chocolate and stir until melted.

Divide the custard between serving dishes. Remove the pears from the oven and put a pear in the centre of each pool of custard. Decorate with strips of lime zest and serve.

INGREDIENTS

115 g/4 oz butter, softened, plus extra
  for greasing
200 g/7 oz soft light brown sugar
2 eggs
3 bananas
225 g/8 oz plain flour
1 tsp bicarbonate of soda
1 tbsp unsweetened cocoa powder
1 tsp mixed spice
125 ml/4 fl oz thick natural yogurt
85 g/3 oz plain dark chocolate chips

chocolate banana *loaf*

SERVES 4–6

Preheat the oven to 180°C/350°F/Gas Mark 4. Grease a 23 x 13 x 7.5-cm/
9 x 5 x 3-inch loaf tin.

Put the butter, sugar and eggs into a bowl and beat well. Peel and mash the
bananas, then add to the mixture. Stir in well. Sift the flour, bicarbonate of
soda, cocoa powder and mixed spice into a separate bowl, then add to the
banana mixture and mix well. Stir in the yogurt and chocolate chips. Spoon
the mixture into the prepared tin and level the surface.

Bake in the oven for 1 hour. To test whether the loaf is cooked through,
insert a skewer into the centre – it should come out clean. If not, return the
loaf to the oven for a few minutes.

INGREDIENTS

3 tbsp butter, plus extra for greasing
2 tbsp caster sugar
2 eggs
6 tbsp plain flour, sifted
1 tsp baking powder, sifted
6 tbsp milk
1 tsp vanilla essence
4 tbsp golden syrup
thin strips of crystallized orange peel,
  to decorate
hot custard, to serve

golden *pudding*

SERVES 4–6

Lightly grease an 850-ml/1½-pint pudding basin. Put the butter into a bowl
with the sugar, and cream together until fluffy. Add the eggs and beat
together well. Mix in the flour and baking powder, then stir in the milk
and vanilla essence. Continue to stir until smooth.

Pour the golden syrup into the pudding basin, then spoon the pudding
mixture on top. Cover with greaseproof paper and top with a piece of
foil, tied on securely with string. Transfer to a large saucepan filled with
enough simmering water to reach halfway up the sides of the pudding
basin. Simmer gently for 1½ hours, or until cooked right through, topping
up with boiling water when necessary.

Lift out the pudding and leave to rest for 5 minutes, then turn it out on to a
serving plate. Decorate with thin strips of crystallized orange peel and serve
with hot custard.

tiramisù

200 ml/7 fl oz strong black coffee, cooled
to room temperature
4 tbsp orange-flavoured liqueur,
such as Cointreau
3 tbsp orange juice
16 Italian sponge fingers
250 g/9 oz mascarpone cheese
300 ml/10 fl oz double cream,
lightly whipped
3 tbsp icing sugar
grated rind of 1 orange
60 g/2¼ oz chocolate, grated

TO DECORATE
chopped toasted almonds
crystallized orange peel

SERVES 4

Pour the cooled coffee into a jug and stir in the liqueur and orange juice. Put 8 of the sponge fingers in the bottom of a serving dish, then pour over half the coffee mixture.

Put the mascarpone cheese in a separate bowl with the cream, sugar and orange rind and mix together well. Spread half the mascarpone mixture over the coffee-soaked sponge fingers, then arrange the remaining sponge fingers on top. Pour over the remaining coffee mixture and then spread over the remaining mascarpone mixture. Scatter over the chocolate, cover and chill in the refrigerator for at least 2 hours.

Serve decorated with chopped toasted almonds and crystallized orange peel.

CHAPTER 4

childhood
favourites

INGREDIENTS

750 g/1 lb 10 oz fresh beef mince
1 beef stock cube
1 tbsp minced dried onion
2 tbsp water
55 g/2 oz grated Cheddar cheese
  (optional)

SERVING SUGGESTIONS
4 sesame buns, toasted
tomato ketchup or chilli sauce
mustard
pickled cucumbers, thinly sliced
Spanish onion, thinly sliced
large tomato, thinly sliced
lettuce leaves
chips

burger & chips

SERVES 4

Place the beef in a large mixing bowl. Crumble the stock cube over the meat, add the dried onion and water and mix well. Divide the meat into 4 portions, shape each into a ball, then flatten slightly to make a burger shape of your preferred thickness.

Preheat a griddle over a high heat. Place the burgers on the griddle and cook for about 5 minutes on each side, depending on how well done you like your meat and the thickness of the burgers. Press down occasionally with a spatula or palette knife during cooking.

To make cheeseburgers, sprinkle the cheese on top of the meat when you have turned it the first time.

Serve the burgers on toasted buns, with a selection of the accompaniments suggested above.

INGREDIENTS

450 g/1 lb floury potatoes, diced
salt and pepper
2 tbsp milk
55 g/2 oz butter, plus extra
  for greasing
225 g/8 oz green cabbage, shredded
225 g/8 oz carrots, thinly sliced
1 onion, chopped
55 g/2 oz Cheddar cheese, grated

bubble & squeak

SERVES 4

Preheat the oven to 190°C/375°F/Gas Mark 5. Cook the potatoes in a
saucepan of lightly salted water for 10 minutes, or until tender. Drain well
and turn into a large mixing bowl. Mash until smooth. Beat with the milk,
half the butter and salt and pepper to taste.

Cook the cabbage and carrots separately in lightly salted water for
5 minutes. Drain well. Mix the cabbage into the potatoes.

Melt the remaining butter in a small frying pan, add the onion and cook
over a medium heat until soft but not brown.

Spread a layer of mashed potato in the bottom of a greased shallow
ovenproof dish. Layer the onion on top, then the carrots. Repeat to use up
all the ingredients, finishing with a layer of potato.

Sprinkle the cheese on top and bake in the oven for 45 minutes, or until the
top is golden and crusty. Remove from the oven and serve immediately.

shepherd's *pie*

INGREDIENTS

900 g/2 lb floury potatoes
salt and pepper
350 g/12 oz cold roast lamb, minced
1 onion, finely chopped
2 tbsp plain flour
1 tbsp tomato purée
300 ml/10 fl oz vegetable stock
2 tbsp chopped fresh parsley,
plus extra to garnish
4 tbsp milk
25 g/1 oz butter

SERVES 4

Preheat the oven to 180°C/350°F/Gas Mark 4.

Cut the potatoes into chunks and cook in a large saucepan of lightly salted water for 15 minutes, or until tender.

Meanwhile, put the lamb, onion, flour, tomato purée, stock, parsley and salt and pepper to taste in a bowl and mix together. Turn out the mixture into an ovenproof dish.

Drain the cooked potatoes, then mash in the saucepan until smooth. Over a low heat, beat in the milk, butter and salt and pepper to taste until well mixed. Spoon on top of the lamb. Mark the top with a fork.

Bake in the oven for 30 minutes, or until golden brown. Garnish with parsley and serve immediately.

INGREDIENTS

2 tbsp vegetable oil

675 g/1 lb 8 oz stewing beef, cubed

3 onions, finely chopped

1 green pepper, deseeded and diced

2 garlic cloves, very finely chopped

2 tbsp tomato purée

2 tbsp plain flour

400 g/14 oz canned chopped tomatoes

250 ml/9 fl oz beef stock

1 fresh bay leaf

3 tbsp chopped fresh parsley

1 tbsp paprika

1 tsp salt

$^{1}/_{4}$ tsp pepper

TO SERVE

buttered noodles

soured cream

beef *goulash*

SERVES 4

Heat the oil in a flameproof casserole over a medium–high heat.
Add the beef and cook until evenly browned. Remove and transfer to a
bowl with a slotted spoon and set aside.

Add the onions and pepper to the casserole and cook, stirring occasionally,
for 5 minutes, or until soft. Add the garlic and cook until just coloured. Stir
in the tomato purée and flour. Cook for 1 minute, stirring constantly.

Return the beef to the casserole. Add the remaining ingredients and bring
to the boil. Cover and simmer over a low heat for 2$^{1}/_{2}$ hours, stirring
occasionally. Add water or more stock if necessary.

Remove the lid and simmer for 15 minutes, stirring to prevent sticking,
until the sauce has thickened and the meat is very tender.

Serve with buttered noodles and a bowl of soured cream.

INGREDIENTS

PASTRY
225 g/8 oz plain wholemeal flour,
   plus extra for dusting
pinch of salt
100 g/3$^{1}/_{2}$ oz butter, diced,
   plus extra for greasing
4 tbsp cold water
2 tbsp milk, for glazing

FILLING
25 g/1 oz butter
1 onion, chopped

125 g/4$^{1}/_{2}$ oz potatoes, chopped
100 g/3$^{1}/_{2}$ oz carrots, chopped
25 g/1 oz French beans, chopped
100 ml/3$^{1}/_{2}$ fl oz water
2 tbsp canned and drained
   sweetcorn kernels
1 tbsp chopped fresh parsley
60 g/2$^{1}/_{4}$ oz Cheddar cheese, grated
salt and pepper

fresh mixed salad, to serve

cheese *&* vegetable *pasties*

SERVES 4

To make the pastry, sift the flour and salt into a large bowl. Rub in the
butter until the mixture resembles breadcrumbs. Add the water and mix
to a dough. Cover with clingfilm. Refrigerate for 40 minutes.

To make the filling, melt the butter in a large saucepan over a low heat.
Add the onion, potatoes and carrots and cook, stirring, for 5 minutes. Add
the French beans and water. Bring to the boil, then reduce the heat and
simmer for 15 minutes. Remove from the heat, drain, rinse under cold
running water, then drain again. Leave to cool.

Preheat the oven to 200°C/400°F/Gas Mark 6. Grease a baking tray. Cut the
pastry into quarters and roll out on a floured work surface into 4 rounds
about 15 cm/6 inches in diameter. Mix the vegetables with the sweetcorn,
parsley, cheese and salt and pepper to taste. Spoon on to one half of each
pastry round. Brush the edges with water, then fold over and press
together. Transfer to the prepared baking tray. Brush all over with milk.
Bake in the oven for 30 minutes, or until golden. Serve with a mixed salad.

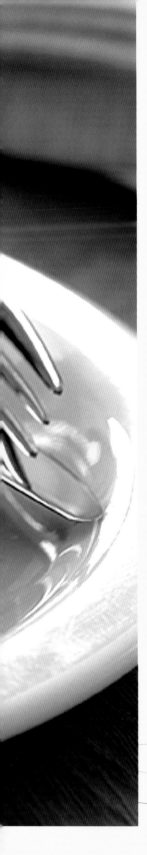

steak & kidney *pie*

INGREDIENTS

**700 g/1 lb 9 oz braising steak, trimmed and
cut into 4-cm/1¹/₂-inch pieces
3 lambs' kidneys, cored and cut into
2.5-cm/1-inch pieces
2 tbsp plain flour, plus extra for dusting
salt and pepper
3 tbsp vegetable oil
1 onion, roughly chopped
1 garlic clove, finely chopped
125 ml/4 fl oz red wine
450 ml/16 fl oz stock
1 bay leaf
butter, for greasing
400 g/14 oz ready-made puff pastry
1 egg, beaten**

SERVES 4–6

Preheat the oven to 160°C/325°F/Gas Mark 3. Put the meat with
the flour and seasoning in a plastic bag and shake until coated.
Heat the oil in a flameproof casserole over a high heat and brown
the meat in batches. Remove with a slotted spoon and keep warm.
Fry the onion and garlic in the casserole for 2–3 minutes until
softened. Stir in the wine and scrape the pan to release the
sediment. Pour in the stock, stirring constantly, and bring to
the boil. Bubble for 2–3 minutes. Add the bay leaf and return
the meat to the casserole. Cover and cook in the oven for
1¹/₂–2 hours. Check the seasoning, then remove the bay leaf.
Leave to cool overnight to develop the flavours.

Preheat the oven to 200°C/400°F/Gas Mark 6. Grease a 1.2-litre/
2-pint pie dish. Roll out the pastry on a lightly floured work
surface to 7 cm/2³/₄ inches larger than the pie dish. Cut off a
3-cm/1¹/₄-inch strip. Moisten the rim and press the pastry strip
onto it. Place a pie funnel in the centre of the dish and spoon
in the filling. Moisten the pastry collar with water and put on
the pastry lid, fitting it around the funnel. Crimp the edges and
glaze with the egg. Place on a tray and cook in the oven for
30 minutes, or until golden brown.

INGREDIENTS

CAKE
butter, for greasing
100 g/3½ oz self-raising flour
pinch of salt
1 tsp mixed spice
½ tsp ground nutmeg
125 g/4½ oz soft light brown sugar
2 eggs, beaten
5 tbsp sunflower oil
125 g/4½ oz carrots, grated
1 banana, chopped
25 g/1 oz chopped toasted mixed nuts

ICING
40 g/1½ oz butter, softened
3 tbsp cream cheese
175 g/6 oz icing sugar, sifted
1 tsp orange juice
grated rind of ½ orange

walnut halves or pieces, to decorate

carrot *cake*

MAKES 6

Preheat the oven to 190°C/375°F/Gas Mark 5. Grease an 18-cm/7-inch square cake tin and line with baking paper. Sift the flour, salt, mixed spice and nutmeg into a bowl. Stir in the brown sugar, then stir in the eggs and oil. Add the carrots, banana and mixed nuts and mix together well.

Spoon the mixture into the prepared cake tin and level the surface. Transfer to the oven and bake for 55 minutes, or until golden and just firm to the touch. Remove from the oven and leave to cool. When cool enough to handle, turn out onto a wire rack and leave to cool completely.

To make the icing, put all the ingredients into a bowl and beat together until creamy. Spread the icing over the top of the cold cake, then use a fork to make shallow wavy lines in the icing. Scatter over the walnuts, cut the cake into bars and serve.

INGREDIENTS

CAKE

175 g/6 oz butter, softened, plus extra
  for greasing
150 g/5½ oz caster sugar
4 eggs, lightly beaten
200 g/7 oz self-raising flour
1 tbsp unsweetened cocoa powder
50 g/1¾ oz plain dark chocolate,
  melted (see page 91)
25 g/1 oz flaked almonds

FILLING

1 tbsp butter, melted
100 g/3½ oz plain dark chocolate,
  melted (see page 91)
275 ml/9½ fl oz double cream
2 tbsp icing sugar, plus extra
  for dusting

chocolate cream sandwich *cake*

SERVES 4–6

Preheat the oven to 190°C/375°F/Gas Mark 5. Grease 2 x 18-cm/7-inch round sandwich tins and line the bases with baking paper.

Put the butter and caster sugar into a bowl and cream until pale and fluffy. Beat in the eggs. Sift the flour and cocoa powder into a separate bowl, then fold into the mixture. Fold in the chocolate. Spoon evenly into the prepared tins, level the surfaces, then scatter the almonds over one of the surfaces only. Bake for 35–40 minutes. Remove from the oven and leave to cool for 10 minutes. Turn out on to a wire rack, discard the lining paper and leave to cool.

To make the filling, stir the butter into the melted chocolate. In a separate bowl, whip the cream until soft peaks form and fold into the chocolate mixture, then stir in the icing sugar. Spread the filling generously on the cake without the almond topping, then place the almond-topped cake carefully on top. Chill in the refrigerator for 1–2 hours, then dust with icing sugar before serving.

banoffee *pie*

INGREDIENTS

2 x 400 ml/14 fl oz cans sweetened
condensed milk
6 tbsp butter, melted, plus extra
for greasing
150 g/5¹/2 oz digestive biscuits,
crushed into crumbs
50 g/1³/4 oz almonds,
toasted and ground
50 g/1³/4 oz shelled hazelnuts,
toasted and ground
4 ripe bananas
1 tbsp lemon juice
1 tsp vanilla essence
75 g/2³/4 oz chocolate, grated
450 ml/16 fl oz thick
double cream, whipped

SERVES 4

Place the cans of milk in a large saucepan and cover them with water. Bring to the boil, then reduce the heat and simmer for 2 hours. Ensure that the water is topped up regularly to keep the cans covered. Carefully lift out the hot cans and leave to cool.

Preheat the oven to 180°C/350°F/Gas Mark 4. Grease a 23-cm/ 9-inch flan tin. Put the butter into a bowl and add the biscuits and nuts. Mix together well, then press the mixture evenly into the base and sides of the flan tin. Bake for 10–12 minutes, then remove from the oven and leave to cool.

Peel and slice the bananas and put them into a bowl. Sprinkle over the lemon juice and vanilla essence and mix gently. Spread the banana mixture over the biscuit crust in the tin, then open the cans of condensed milk and spoon the contents over the bananas. Sprinkle over 50 g/1³/4 oz of the chocolate, then top with a thick layer of whipped cream. Scatter over the remaining chocolate and serve.

chocolate chip *muffins*

INGREDIENTS

100 g/3¹/₂ oz butter, softened
125 g/4¹/₂ oz caster sugar
100 g/3¹/₂ oz dark muscovado sugar
2 eggs
150 ml/5 fl oz soured cream
5 tbsp milk
250 g/9 oz plain flour
1 tsp bicarbonate of soda
2 tbsp unsweetened cocoa powder
190 g/6¹/₂ oz plain dark chocolate chips

MAKES 12

Preheat the oven to 190°C/375°F/Gas Mark 5. Line a 12-cup muffin tin with paper cases.

Put the butter, caster sugar and dark muscovado sugar into a bowl and beat well. Beat in the eggs, cream and milk until thoroughly mixed. Sift the flour, bicarbonate of soda and cocoa powder into a separate bowl and stir into the mixture. Add the chocolate chips and mix well. Spoon the mixture into the paper cases. Bake in the oven for 25–30 minutes.

Remove from the oven and leave to cool for 10 minutes. Turn out onto a wire rack and leave to cool completely. Store in an airtight container until required.

INGREDIENTS

90 g/3¹/4 oz butter or margarine,
  plus extra for greasing
55 g/2 oz muscovado sugar
5 tbsp black treacle
1 egg white
1 tsp almond essence
175 g/6 oz plain flour,
  plus extra for dusting
¹/4 tsp bicarbonate of soda

¹/4 tsp baking powder
pinch of salt
¹/2 tsp mixed spice
¹/2 tsp ground ginger
125 g/4¹/2 oz dessert apples, cooked
  and finely chopped

gingerbread *squares*

MAKES 24

Preheat the oven to 180°C/350°F/Gas Mark 4. Grease a large baking tray
and line it with baking paper. Put the butter, sugar, treacle, egg white and
almond essence into a food processor and blend until smooth.

In a separate bowl, sift the flour, bicarbonate of soda, baking powder, salt,
mixed spice and ginger together. Add to the creamed mixture and beat
together thoroughly. Stir in the chopped apples. Pour the mixture onto
the prepared baking tray.

Transfer to the oven and bake for 10 minutes, or until golden brown.
Remove from the oven and cut into 24 pieces. Transfer the squares to a
wire rack and let them cool completely before serving.

INGREDIENTS

70 g/2¹/2 oz plain dark chocolate,
  chopped
140 g/5 oz plain flour
³/4 tsp bicarbonate of soda
¹/4 tsp baking powder
225 g/8 oz unsalted butter,
  plus extra for greasing

100 g/3¹/2 oz demerara sugar
¹/2 tsp almond essence
1 egg
1 tsp milk
55 g/2 oz shelled pecan nuts,
  finely chopped

pecan *brownies*

MAKES 20

Preheat the oven to 180°C/350°F/Gas Mark 4. Grease a large baking tray
and line it with baking paper.

Put the chocolate into a heatproof bowl over a saucepan of barely
simmering water (a double boiler is ideal) and heat until it is melted.
While the chocolate is melting, sift the flour, bicarbonate of soda and
baking powder together into a large bowl.

In a separate bowl, cream the butter and sugar together, then mix in the
almond essence and the egg. Remove the chocolate from the heat and stir
into the butter mixture. Add the flour mixture, milk and chopped nuts to
the bowl and stir until well combined.

Spoon the mixture onto the prepared baking tray and level it. Transfer to
the oven and bake for 30 minutes, or until firm to the touch (it should still
be a little gooey in the centre). Remove from the oven and leave to cool
completely. Cut into 20 squares and serve.

fruit *pancakes*

INGREDIENTS

PANCAKES
125 g/4¹/₂ oz plain flour
pinch of salt
2 eggs
300 ml/10 fl oz milk
2–3 tbsp vegetable oil

FILLING
1 banana
1 tbsp lemon juice
2 nectarines, stoned and
cut into small pieces
1 mango, peeled, stoned and
cut into small pieces
3 kiwi fruit, peeled and
cut into small pieces
2 tbsp maple syrup

icing sugar, for dusting
whipped cream, to serve

SERVES 4

To make the pancakes, sift the flour and salt into a bowl. Whisk in the eggs and milk. Cover with clingfilm and chill for 30 minutes.

To make the filling, peel and slice the banana and put into a large bowl. Pour over the lemon juice and stir gently until coated. Add the nectarines, mango, kiwi fruit and maple syrup and stir together gently until mixed.

Heat a little oil in a frying pan until hot. Remove the pancake batter from the refrigerator and add a large spoonful to the pan. Cook over a high heat until golden, then turn over and cook briefly on the other side. Remove from the pan and keep warm. Cook the other pancakes in the same way, stacking them on a plate. Keep warm. Divide the fruit filling between the pancakes and fold into triangles or roll into horns. Dust with icing sugar and serve with whipped cream.

CHAPTER 5

chocolate *therapy*

INGREDIENTS

CAKE
butter, for greasing
125 g/4^1/$_2$ oz plain dark chocolate,
  chopped
50 g/1^3/$_4$ oz Continental plain dark
  chocolate, chopped
3 tbsp warm water
2 tbsp coffee-flavoured liqueur,
  such as Kahlúa (optional)
5 eggs, separated
175 g/6 oz caster sugar

FILLING
450 ml/16 fl oz double cream
40 g/1^1/$_2$ oz icing sugar, sifted, plus
  extra for dusting
20 g/^{3}/$_4$ oz unsweetened
  cocoa powder
2 tsp espresso coffee powder,
  dissolved in 1 tbsp boiling water

halved strawberries, to decorate

rich chocolate *roulade*

SERVES 4–6

Preheat the oven to 180°C/350°F/Gas Mark 4. Grease and line a
35 x 25-cm/14 x 10-inch Swiss roll tin.

Put the chocolate into a heatproof bowl and set over a saucepan of hot
water, stirring occasionally, until melted. Stir in the water and liqueur, if
using. Whisk the egg yolks and caster sugar in a separate bowl until pale.
Beat the chocolate into the yolk mixture. Whisk the egg whites in another
bowl until stiff, then fold into the chocolate mixture. Pour into the
prepared tin and bake for 15 minutes. Remove, cover with greaseproof
paper and leave to cool for 3–4 hours. Meanwhile, whisk all the filling
ingredients together in a bowl until thick. Cover with clingfilm and chill.

Turn out the cake onto greaseproof paper dusted with icing sugar. Discard
the lining paper. Reserve 4 tablespoons of the filling, then spread the rest
over the roulade, leaving a 2.5-cm/1-inch border. Starting from a short
side, roll up the cake. Discard the paper. Pipe the remaining filling on top,
decorate with strawberries and serve.

INGREDIENTS

100 g/3¹/₂ oz stoned dates, chopped

50 g/1³/₄ oz raisins

50 g/1³/₄ oz sultanas

1 tsp almond extract

40 g/1¹/₂ oz plain dark chocolate,
  melted (see page 91)

8 slices day-old white or wholemeal
  bread, crusts removed

3 eggs

2 tbsp almond-flavoured liqueur,
  such as Amaretto

275 ml/9¹/₂ fl oz milk

85 g/3 oz plain dark chocolate, grated

25 g/1 oz flaked almonds

¹/₂ tsp mixed spice

double cream, to serve

chocolate bread *pudding*

SERVES 4

Preheat the oven to 180°C/350°F/Gas Mark 4.

Put the dates, raisins and sultanas into a large bowl, pour over the almond
extract and set aside to soak. Spread the melted chocolate evenly over one
side of each slice of bread, then cut each slice in half diagonally and then
again to make 4 triangles. Arrange half the triangles in a layer in the base
of an ovenproof dish, then spoon over the fruit with the almond extract.
Arrange the remaining bread triangles in a layer over the top.

Put the eggs and liqueur into a heatproof bowl and beat well. Heat the
milk and chocolate in a saucepan over a low heat, stirring, until melted
and hot, but not boiling. Remove from the heat and stir into the beaten
eggs. Pour over the bread pudding, then top with the almonds. Sprinkle
over the mixed spice.

Bake in the oven for 30 minutes, or until risen. Remove from the oven and
serve with generous spoonfuls of cream.

chocolate cherry *gâteau*

INGREDIENTS

900 g/2 lb fresh cherries, stoned and halved
250 g/9 oz caster sugar
100 ml/3$\frac{1}{2}$ fl oz cherry brandy
100 g/3$\frac{1}{2}$ oz plain flour
50 g/1$\frac{3}{4}$ oz cocoa powder
$\frac{1}{2}$ tsp baking powder
4 eggs
3 tbsp unsalted butter, melted, plus extra
for greasing
1 litre/1$\frac{3}{4}$ pints double cream

TO DECORATE
grated plain dark chocolate
whole fresh cherries

SERVES 4 – 6

Preheat the oven to 180°C/350°F/Gas Mark 4. Grease and line a 23-cm/9-inch springform cake tin. Put the cherries into a saucepan with 3 tablespoons of the sugar and the cherry brandy. Simmer for 5 minutes. Drain, reserving the syrup. In a bowl, sift the flour, cocoa powder and baking powder together.

Put the eggs into a heatproof bowl and beat in 160 g/5$\frac{3}{4}$ oz of the remaining sugar. Place the bowl over a saucepan of barely simmering water and beat for 6 minutes, or until thickened. Remove from the heat, then gradually fold in the flour mixture and melted butter. Spoon into the prepared cake tin. Bake for 40 minutes. Remove from the oven and leave to cool. Turn out the cake and cut in half horizontally. Whip the cream with the remaining sugar until peaks form. Spread the reserved syrup over the cut sides of the cake. Arrange the cherries over one half, top with a layer of cream and place the other half on top. Cover the whole cake with cream, press grated chocolate all over and decorate with cherries.

INGREDIENTS

BASE
115 g/4 oz digestive biscuits,
  finely crushed
2 tsp unsweetened cocoa powder
4 tbsp butter, melted, plus extra
  for greasing

CHOCOLATE LAYER
800 g/1 lb 12 oz mascarpone cheese
200 g/7 oz icing sugar, sifted

juice of $^1/_2$ orange
finely grated rind of 1 orange
175 g/6 oz plain dark chocolate,
  melted (see page 91)
2 tbsp brandy

TO DECORATE
Chocolate Leaves (see page 110)
halved kumquats

deep chocolate *cheesecake*

SERVES 4–6

Grease a 20-cm/8-inch loose-bottomed cake tin.

To make the base, put the crushed biscuits, cocoa powder and melted butter into a large bowl and mix well. Press the biscuit mixture evenly over the base of the prepared tin.

Put the mascarpone cheese and sugar into a bowl and stir in the orange juice and rind. Add the melted chocolate and brandy and mix together until thoroughly combined. Spread the chocolate mixture evenly over the biscuit layer. Cover with clingfilm and chill for at least 4 hours.

Remove the cheesecake from the refrigerator, turn out onto a serving platter and decorate with Chocolate Leaves (see page 110) and kumquat halves. Serve immediately.

INGREDIENTS

4 trifle sponges

4 tbsp cherry brandy

425 g/15 oz canned cherries, drained

2 egg yolks

3 tbsp caster sugar

2 tbsp cornflour

1 tbsp unsweetened cocoa powder

350 ml/12 fl oz milk

150 ml/5 fl oz single cream

140 g/5 oz plain dark chocolate, grated

175 ml/6 fl oz double cream

whole fresh cherries, to decorate

dark chocolate *trifle*

SERVES 4

Break the trifle sponges into small pieces and arrange in the base of a large glass serving bowl. Pour over the cherry brandy and arrange the cherries on top.

In a heatproof bowl, beat the egg yolks, then beat in the sugar, cornflour and cocoa powder. Heat the milk and single cream in a saucepan over a low heat, stirring, until just starting to boil. Remove from the heat, then whisk into the egg mixture. Return the mixture to a clean saucepan and cook over a low heat, stirring, until thickened and smooth. Add half the chocolate and stir until melted. Remove from the heat and leave to cool to room temperature. Pour the custard over the cherries, cover with clingfilm and chill for at least 8 hours or overnight.

Whip the double cream in a bowl until peaks form. Spoon a layer over the trifle, then sprinkle over the remaining chocolate and cherries. Serve immediately, or cover with clingfilm and chill until required.

rich chocolate *mousses*

INGREDIENTS

300 g/10^1/$_2$ oz plain dark chocolate
(at least 70% cocoa solids)
1^1/$_2$ tbsp unsalted butter
1 tbsp brandy
4 eggs, separated
cocoa powder, for dusting

SERVES 4

Break the chocolate into small pieces and put into a heatproof bowl set over a saucepan of barely simmering water. Add the butter and melt with the chocolate, stirring, until smooth. Remove from the heat, stir in the brandy and allow to cool a little. Add the egg yolks and beat until smooth.

In a separate bowl, whisk the egg whites until stiff peaks have formed, then fold into the chocolate mixture. Divide 4 stainless steel cooking rings between 4 small serving plates, then spoon the mixture into each ring and level the surfaces. Transfer to the refrigerator and chill for at least 4 hours until set.

Remove the mousses from the refrigerator and discard the cooking rings. Dust with cocoa powder and serve.

INGREDIENTS

250 g/9 oz plain dark chocolate
  (at least 50% cocoa solids)
100 ml/3¹/₂ fl oz double cream
2 tbsp brandy

DIPPERS
plain sponge cake, cut into
  bite-sized pieces
small pink and white marshmallows
small firm whole fresh fruits, such as
  blackcurrants, blueberries, cherries
  and strawberries
whole no-soak dried apricots
crystallized citrus peel,
  cut decoratively into strips
  or bite-sized pieces

deep chocolate *fondue*

SERVES 4

Arrange the dippers decoratively on a serving platter or individual
serving plates and set aside.

Break or chop the chocolate into small pieces and place in the top of
a double boiler or in a heatproof bowl set over a saucepan of barely
simmering water. Pour in the cream and stir until melted and smooth.
Stir in the brandy, then carefully pour the mixture into a warmed
fondue pot.

Using protective gloves, transfer the fondue pot to a lit tabletop burner.
To serve, invite your guests to spear the dippers onto fondue forks and
dip them into the fondue.

INGREDIENTS

16 wonton wrappers
350 g/12 oz plain dark chocolate,
  chopped
1 tbsp cornflour
3 tbsp cold water
1 litre/1³/₄ pints groundnut oil

MAPLE SAUCE
175 ml/6 fl oz maple syrup
4 tbsp butter
¹/₂ tsp mixed spice

vanilla ice cream, to serve

chocolate *wontons*
with maple sauce

SERVES 4

Spread out the wonton wrappers on a clean work surface, then spoon a
little chopped chocolate into the centre of each wrapper. In a small bowl,
mix the cornflour and water together until smooth. Brush the edges of the
wrappers with the cornflour mixture, then wrap in any preferred shape,
such as triangles, squares or bundles, and seal the edges. Arrange the
wontons on a serving platter.

To make the maple sauce, put all the ingredients into a saucepan and stir
over a medium heat. Bring to the boil, then reduce the heat and simmer
for 3 minutes.

Meanwhile, pour the oil into a metal fondue pot (it should be no more than
one-third full). Heat on the hob to 190°C/375°F, or until a cube of bread
browns in 30 seconds. Using protective gloves, transfer the fondue pot to
a lit tabletop burner. To serve, invite your guests to place the wontons on
metal spoons and dip them into the hot oil until cooked (they will need
about 2–3 minutes). Drain off the excess oil. Serve with vanilla ice cream
and the sauce.

rich chocolate *fudge*

INGREDIENTS

50 g/1³/4 oz raisins
2 tbsp rum
150 ml/5 fl oz milk
450 g/1 lb caster sugar
3 tbsp unsalted butter, diced,
plus extra for greasing
100 g/3¹/2 oz plain dark chocolate,
broken into small pieces
50 g/1³/4 oz shelled pistachio nuts,
chopped

SERVES 4

Grease a 20-cm/8-inch square baking tin.

Put the raisins in a bowl, pour over the rum and set aside.

Heat the milk and sugar in a saucepan over a low heat, stirring, until the sugar has dissolved. Add the butter and chocolate and stir until melted. Add the pistachio nuts and the rum-soaked raisins and mix well. Bring gently to the boil, then cook over a medium heat, stirring constantly, for 15–20 minutes.

Remove the fudge from the heat, press evenly into the prepared tin and level the surface. Leave to cool completely, then cover with clingfilm and chill for at least 1 hour, or until firm. Remove from the refrigerator, turn out onto a chopping board and cut into squares. Return to the refrigerator until required.

To serve, remove from the refrigerator and arrange on a serving plate, in paper cases if desired.

120 g/4^{1}/$_{4}$ oz white chocolate,
   broken into small, even-sized pieces
4 tbsp butter, softened to
   room temperature
2 tbsp double cream
^{1}/$_{2}$ tsp brandy
grated white chocolate, to decorate

white chocolate *truffles*

MAKES 20

Put the chocolate pieces into a heatproof glass bowl and place over a
saucepan of hot but not simmering water. When it starts to melt, stir gently
until completely melted. Do not overheat, or the chocolate will separate.
Remove from the heat and gently stir in the butter, then the cream and
brandy. Leave to cool, then cover with clingfilm and refrigerate for
2–2^{1}/$_{2}$ hours, or until set.

Remove the chocolate mixture from the refrigerator. Using a teaspoon,
scoop out small pieces of the mixture, then use your hands to roll them into
balls. To decorate, roll the balls in grated white chocolate. To store, transfer
to an airtight container and refrigerate for up to 12 days.

INGREDIENTS

365 g/12¹/₂ oz plain dark chocolate
6 tbsp unsalted butter, plus extra
  for greasing
1 tsp strong coffee
2 eggs
140 g/5 oz light muscovado sugar
215 g/7¹/₂ oz plain flour
¹/₄ tsp baking powder
pinch of salt

2 tsp almond essence
115 g/4 oz shelled Brazil nuts,
  chopped
115 g/4 oz shelled hazelnuts, chopped
40 g/1¹/₂ oz white chocolate

chocolate temptations

MAKES 24

Preheat the oven to 180°C/350°F/Gas Mark 4. Grease a large baking sheet.
Put 225 g/8 oz of the plain dark chocolate with the butter and coffee into a
heatproof bowl set over a saucepan of barely simmering water and heat
until the chocolate is almost melted.

Meanwhile, beat the eggs in a bowl until fluffy. Whisk in the sugar
gradually until thick. Remove the chocolate mixture from the heat and stir
until smooth. Stir into the egg mixture until combined.

Sift the flour, baking powder and salt into a separate bowl and stir into the
chocolate mixture. Chop 85 g/3 oz of the remaining plain dark chocolate
into pieces and stir into the mixture. Stir in the almond essence and nuts.

Put 24 rounded dessertspoonfuls of the mixture onto the prepared baking
sheet and bake for 16 minutes. Transfer to a wire rack to cool.

To decorate, melt the remaining plain dark chocolate and white chocolate
in turn, spoon into a piping bag and pipe lines onto the biscuits.

white chocolate *cake*

INGREDIENTS

CAKE
butter, for greasing
4 eggs
125 g/4¹/₂ oz caster sugar
125 g/4¹/₂ oz plain flour, sifted
pinch of salt
300 ml/10 fl oz double cream
150 g/5¹/₂ oz white chocolate, chopped

CHOCOLATE LEAVES
75 g/2³/₄ oz plain dark or white chocolate,
melted (see page 91)
handful of rose leaves, or other small edible
leaves with well-defined veins,
washed and dried

SERVES 4–6

To make the chocolate leaves, brush the melted chocolate over the undersides of the leaves. Arrange, coated-sides up, on a baking sheet lined with baking paper. Chill until set, then peel away the leaves.

Preheat the oven to 180°C/350°F/Gas Mark 4. Grease and line a 20-cm/8-inch round cake tin. Put the eggs and sugar into a heatproof bowl and set over a saucepan of simmering water. Whisk until thick, remove from the heat and whisk until cool. Fold in the flour and salt. Pour into the prepared tin and bake for 20 minutes, then cool for 10 minutes. Turn out, discard the lining paper and leave to cool.

Put the cream into a saucepan over a low heat and bring to the boil, stirring. Add the chocolate and stir until melted. Pour into a bowl, cover with clingfilm and chill overnight.

Cut the cake horizontally in half. Whisk the chocolate cream until thick, spread one-third over one half of the cake and top with the other half. Coat with the remaining chocolate cream. Chill for 1–2 hours, decorate with chocolate leaves and serve.